Ketanji Brown Jackson Biography

Breaking Barriers
in the Highest Court

By
Margaret M. Doyle

Table of Content

Introduction

In the vast expanse of American history, few figures have risen to prominence with the same combination of intellect, perseverance, and unyielding commitment to justice as Ketanji Brown Jackson. Her journey to the United States Supreme Court is not just the story of an individual breaking barriers; it is the story of a nation grappling with its ideals and the evolving interpretation of those ideals through the lens of the law. From the moment President Joe Biden announced her nomination, Jackson's ascent has symbolized more than just a personal achievement, it has marked a pivotal moment in the ongoing quest for equity and representation within the highest echelons of American power.

Jackson's nomination to the Supreme Court was a landmark event for her and the many Americans who recognized in her a mirror of their difficulties and ambitions. It was a moment that brought with it the weight of history—both the burden of past injustices and the promise of a more inclusive future. As the first Black woman chosen to the Supreme Court, Jackson's presence on the bench disrupts the established quo and reshapes the narrative of what is possible in America.

However, to properly comprehend the importance of Ketanji Brown Jackson's position on the Supreme Court, one must first understand her route to get there—a path defined by hardships that would have discouraged many but only increased her drive. Born in Washington, D.C., and reared in Miami, Florida, Jackson grew up in an idealistic yet bitterly divided society. The civil rights movement had made considerable achievements. However, structural racism and inequality were still widespread. It was within this atmosphere that Jackson's persona was forged—one that her passion for justice and equality would define.

Her early life was immersed in the principles of education, public service, and a steadfast conviction in the power of the law to create change. Jackson's brilliance and dedication set her apart as she succeeded academically, first at Miami Palmetto Senior High School and subsequently at Harvard University. Yet, her stay at Harvard Law School affected her legal perspective. Here, she sharpened her talents as a legal scholar and started to acquire the empathy and understanding that would become characteristics of her judicial career.

A sequence of firsts and breakthrough accomplishments have distinguished Jackson's career. As a public defender, she stood at the forefront of the judicial system, arguing for individuals who could not afford to defend themselves. This encounter offered her a distinct viewpoint she would carry throughout her career. In a system frequently criticized for its biases and injustices, Jackson's work as a public defender testified to her conviction in the fundamental right to a fair trial and the significance of offering a voice to the voiceless.

Her service on the U.S. Sentencing Commission further reinforced her image as a knowledgeable and ethical champion for justice. Here, she played a significant role in changing federal sentencing rules, notably in addressing the racial inequities that had long plagued the criminal justice system. Jackson's work on the Commission was marked by her rigorous attention to detail and uncompromising devotion to justice, hallmarks of her later judicial career.

When Jackson was first appointed to the U.S. District Court for the District of Columbia and then to the U.S. Court of Appeals for the D.C. Circuit, she brought a depth of expertise and a firm grasp of the law's effect on ordinary lives. Her verdicts were defined by a delicate mix of legal rigor and human empathy, reflecting her view that the law must be implemented accurately and compassionately. This strategy garnered her respect across the political spectrum and eventually led to her historic nomination to the Supreme Court.

As a Supreme Court Justice, Jackson's impact exceeds her opinions. Her presence on the Court undermines the ingrained norms of the American judiciary. It symbolizes progress for individuals who have long been underrepresented in the corridors of power. Her judicial philosophy, molded by a lifetime of activism and a profound dedication to justice, continues to drive her choices, ensuring that the Court represents the many perspectives and beliefs of the American people.

In the following pages, we will explore Ketanji Brown Jackson's life and career, analyzing the crucial experiences that have defined her path and the legacy she is establishing on the Supreme Court. This is not merely a narrative of legal milestones and historic successes; it is the story of a woman who, through her brilliance, determination, and unrelenting devotion to justice, is working to transform the fabric of American society.

Chapter 1

Growing up

Ketanji Brown Jackson's story begins in an environment rich with the pursuit of knowledge and the power of education. Born in Washington, D.C., on September 14, 1970, Ketanji was raised in an environment that valued education and was ingrained in her childhood. Her parents were Johnny and Ellery Brown. Johnny Brown, her father, had a unique career path that led him from teaching history to becoming the Miami-Dade County School Board's head counsel. His commitment to education and justice influenced young Ketanji, shaping her aspirations and instilling a deep respect for the law.

Ellery Brown, Ketanji's mother, was equally impactful. As the principal of the New World School of the Arts in Miami, she set high academic standards and fostered a creative environment that nurtured her students' artistic talents. Ellery's dedication to education extended beyond the school walls; she was a constant source of support and inspiration for her daughter, always encouraging her to strive for excellence.

Growing up in Miami, Ketanji was surrounded by a vibrant community that challenged and supported her. The Brown family's involvement in education meant that Ketanji was acutely aware of the disparities in educational opportunities, particularly for Black students in the South. These observations would later fuel her commitment to justice and equity.

Her extraordinary intellectual curiosity marked Ketanji's childhood. Even as a young girl, she was an avid reader, devouring books far beyond her age. Her parents encouraged this passion, providing her a home filled with literature and discussions about history, law, and society. This intellectual environment was complemented by the cultural diversity of Miami, where Ketanji was exposed to various perspectives that enriched her understanding of the world.

At Miami Palmetto Senior High School, Ketanji's talents blossomed further. She excelled academically and became a star debater, a skill that later proved invaluable in her legal career. Her ability to argue persuasively and her quick wit made her a formidable opponent in debate competitions. These experiences in high school honed her public speaking skills and solidified her interest in pursuing a career in law.

One pivotal moment in her early life was her participation in the National Catholic Forensic League (NCFL) Championships in New Orleans, where she won the national oratory title. This victory proved her skills and reflected her growing confidence in her abilities to make a difference through the power of words and reasoned argument.

Ketanji's upbringing in a family that valued education above all else and her early successes in academia and debate set the stage for her future endeavours. Her parents' influence, coupled with her determination, laid the foundation for a career that would define a relentless pursuit of justice and equality. The lessons she learned from her family—about the importance of education, perseverance, and the need to fight for what is right—would guide her throughout her life and career.

Harvard Years

When Ketanji Brown Jackson arrived at Harvard College in the late 1980s, she stepped into an exhilarating and intimidating world. For a young woman who had grown up in a predominantly Black community in Miami, the stark contrast of Harvard's predominantly white, elite environment was a challenge she was determined to overcome. Harvard was a place where the intellectual rigour was intense, and the competition was fierce. Yet, Ketanji was not one to be daunted.

Her first year at Harvard was marked by a significant and formative experience. During her first year, she witnessed a student display a Confederate flag in a dormitory window. This incident was a stark reminder of the racial tensions that still existed, even in a place as prestigious as Harvard. Rather than retreat, Ketanji chose to confront the situation. She became involved in student activism, speaking out against racism and advocating for greater diversity and inclusion on campus. This experience was pivotal, reinforcing her commitment to social justice and preparing her for the challenges she would face later in her career.

Ketanji's academic journey at Harvard was nothing short of remarkable. She excelled in her studies, graduating magna cum laude with a degree in Government in 1992. Her time at Harvard was not just about academics; it was also where she honed her leadership skills. She became a prominent figure in the Black Students Association and other campus organizations, using these platforms to advocate for marginalized communities.

After completing her undergraduate degree, Ketanji returned to Harvard to pursue a law degree. Harvard Law School was another crucible, where she was tested by the demanding curriculum and the high expectations of her professors and peers. Here, she would develop the legal understanding that would define her career.

Her position as editor of the esteemed Harvard Law Review was one of the most significant achievements of her career at Harvard Law. The Law Review was an incubator for some of the nation's brightest legal minds, and Ketanji's selection as an editor was proof of her exceptional abilities. The work was gruelling, involving long research, writing, and editing hours, but it was also gratifying. As an editor, she was responsible for reviewing and critiquing legal scholarship. This assignment called for a thorough knowledge of the law as well as the capacity for critical thought and strong argumentation.

Her experience at the Law Review shaped her approach to the law. It taught her the importance of precision, clarity, and rigour in legal writing—skills that would become hallmarks of her judicial opinions. Moreover, it gave her the confidence to know that she could hold her own in the highest echelons of the legal profession.

Ketanji's time at Harvard was also marked by a deepening of her personal beliefs and values. The challenges she faced, both academically and socially, reinforced her commitment to justice and equality. She understood that the law was not just an abstract set of rules but a powerful tool that could be used to effect real change in people's lives. This belief would guide her throughout her career, from her early days as a public defender to her eventual rise to the Supreme Court.

As she graduated from Harvard Law School in 1996, cum laude, Ketanji Brown Jackson was not just a young lawyer; she was a woman with a mission. The experiences, challenges, and triumphs of her time at Harvard had prepared her for the road ahead. She was ready to take on the world, armed with the knowledge, skills, and values that would define her career and her contributions to law.

Chapter 2

Mentors

As Ketanji Brown Jackson stepped into the world of law after completing her education at Harvard Law School, she was acutely aware that the path ahead would be challenging yet filled with opportunities to make a meaningful impact. Her legal journey began with clerkships—an essential rite of passage for many young lawyers. These early years were not merely about learning the intricacies of the law but about shaping her identity as a legal professional, absorbing wisdom from seasoned judges, and understanding the real-world application of legal principles.

Her first clerkship was with The District of Massachusetts U.S. District Court Judge Patti B. Saris. Working under Judge Saris offered Ketanji a hands-on introduction to the judiciary, where she was exposed to the complexities of federal law. Judge Saris, known for her meticulous attention to detail and her commitment to fairness, became an early mentor to Ketanji. The experience deepened her understanding of how judicial decisions can affect people's lives. Saris's approach to the law—balancing empathy with a rigorous analysis of legal texts—resonated with Ketanji and influenced her future judicial philosophy.

The next step in her career took her to the U.S. Court of Appeals for the First Circuit, where she clerked for Judge Bruce M. Selya. This experience further honed her legal reasoning and writing skills. Judge Selya was known for his elegant and concise opinions, and under his mentorship, Ketanji developed a keen appreciation for the craft of legal writing. Selya's emphasis on clarity and precision became a hallmark of Ketanji's later work, particularly in her judicial opinions. During this time, she also began to see the broader implications of appellate decisions, as these rulings often set precedents that shaped the interpretation of law across the nation.

However, the most significant of her clerkships was her time with Justice Stephen Breyer of the U.S. Supreme Court. Clerking for a Supreme Court Justice is a prestigious position reserved for the most promising young legal minds. Ketanji's selection was proof of her outstanding academic and professional achievements. Under Justice Breyer's guidance, Ketanji was introduced to the highest level of legal reasoning and the complexities of constitutional law. Breyer, known for his pragmatic approach to the law, encouraged Ketanji to think deeply about the real-world consequences of judicial decisions. His influence can be seen in her later judicial philosophy, which often reflects a careful consideration of legal principles and their impact on society.

During her time with Justice Breyer, Ketanji was also exposed to the inner workings of the Supreme Court. She gained first-hand experience in the justices' deliberative processes, observing how they debated and decided on some of the most significant legal issues of the time. This experience was invaluable, as it gave her insights into the balancing act that Justices must perform— adhering to the Constitution and adapting legal principles to contemporary societal needs.

These clerkships were more than just professional stepping stones; they were formative experiences that shaped Ketanji's approach to the law. Through her mentors, she learned the importance of judicial independence, the need for meticulous legal analysis, and the responsibility of interpreting the law. These experiences contributed to her development as a legal professional, setting the stage for her future public service and judiciary roles.

Private Practice and Public Service

After her clerkships, Ketanji Brown Jackson transitioned into private practice, allowing her to apply the skills she had honed in a new context. She joined the Boston office of a prestigious law firm, where she worked on various civil and criminal cases. The fast-paced environment of private practice was a stark contrast to her clerkships, but it offered her a different perspective on the law—one that was rooted in the realities of representing clients with diverse legal needs.

In private practice, Ketanji was known for her thorough preparation and her ability to craft persuasive arguments. In addition to handling complicated lawsuits and often defending big businesses, she worked on pro bono matters, giving individuals in need of legal assistance access to them. This duality—working in the high-stakes world of corporate law while also serving the underprivileged- symbolized her broader legal philosophy. She thought that everyone should be able to access the law, regardless of their financial situation or background.

However, it was only a short time before Ketanji felt the pull of public service. While rewarding, her experiences in private practice did not fully align with her desire to make a broader impact on society. The turning point came when she was offered a position as a federal public defender in Washington, D.C. This role marked a significant shift in her career as she moved from representing corporate clients to defending individuals often marginalized by the legal system.

As a federal public defender, Ketanji represented indigent clients, many of whom faced severe criminal charges. This work was challenging, both emotionally and intellectually, but it was also deeply fulfilling. She fought tirelessly for her clients, often going up against the total weight of the federal government. Her time as a public defender shaped her understanding of the criminal justice system and deepened her commitment to ensuring that all individuals received fair representation, regardless of their circumstances.

One of the most significant aspects of her work as a public defender was her involvement in cases related to detainees held at Guantanamo Bay. These highly controversial cases placed Ketanji at the centre of national debates about human rights and national security. Despite the intense scrutiny, she remained steadfast in her belief that even those accused of the most heinous crimes deserved a robust defence. Her work in these cases demonstrated her courage and unwavering commitment to justice principles.

Ketanji's experience as a public defender was not just about defending clients but also about understanding the systemic issues that contributed to their circumstances. She became acutely aware of the disparities in the criminal justice system, particularly how race and socioeconomic status could influence outcomes. This awareness would later inform her work on the U.S. Sentencing Commission, where she would advocate for more equitable sentencing practices.

While her time in private practice and as a public defender was crucial in shaping her legal philosophy, they also highlighted the broader systemic issues within the legal system. These experiences fueled her desire to transition into roles where she could influence public policy and advocate for justice on a larger scale. This drive eventually led her to the U.S. Sentencing Commission, where she would continue her work on ensuring fairness and equity in the legal system.

Chapter 3

Champion of Justice

When Ketanji Brown Jackson joined the U.S. Sentencing Commission in 2010, she stepped into a role that would allow her to influence federal sentencing practices at a national level. Appointed as Vice Chair by President Barack Obama, Jackson was tasked with addressing some of the most critical issues facing the U.S. criminal justice system. Her work at the Commission was characterized by a relentless focus on fairness, equity, and reducing disparities that had long plagued federal sentencing.

From the outset, Jackson's approach was pragmatic yet deeply empathetic. She understood that sentencing decisions had profound implications for the individuals involved and society as a whole. One of her key priorities was to address the longstanding disparities in sentencing for drug offences, particularly those involving crack cocaine. At the time, the sentencing guidelines imposed significantly harsher penalties for crack cocaine offences compared to those involving powder cocaine, a disparity that disproportionately affected Black communities.

Jackson was pivotal in the Commission's efforts to reduce this disparity. The Fair Punishment Act, approved by Congress in 2010, decreased the punishment ratio from 100:1 for crack cocaine to 18:1 for powder cocaine. Jackson and the Sentencing Commission were instrumental in pushing these changes to be applied retroactively, allowing thousands of individuals serving disproportionately long sentences to seek reductions. This move was not without controversy, but Jackson's advocacy was driven by a commitment to justice and the belief that the law should be applied equitably to all.

Another significant area of focus for Jackson was the sentencing guidelines related to mandatory minimums. She was acutely aware of how mandatory minimum sentences often stripped judges of the discretion needed to consider the individual circumstances of each case. Jackson worked with the Commission to recommend changes that would allow for greater judicial flexibility, particularly in cases where the mandatory minimums were deemed excessively harsh or unjust. Her efforts were part of a broader movement towards sentencing reform that sought to balance the need for public safety with the principles of justice and fairness.

Jackson's tenure at the Sentencing Commission was also marked by her work on sentencing for economic crimes. Recognizing the complexity of these offences and the varying degrees of harm they caused, she advocated for more nuanced guidelines allowing judges to impose sentences that better reflect each case's specifics. This reflected her broader belief in the importance of judicial discretion and the need for fair and proportionate sentencing.

Throughout her time at the Commission, Jackson was known for her meticulous attention to detail and ability to navigate complex legal issues. She was a consensus-builder, often working behind the scenes to bring together different stakeholders and ensure that the Commission's recommendations were practical and just. Her work was guided by a deep understanding of the human impact of sentencing decisions, and she was committed to ensuring that the Commission's guidelines reflected the values of fairness and equity.

Jackson's contributions to the U.S. Sentencing Commission had a lasting impact on federal sentencing practices. Her efforts to reduce disparities and promote fairness in sentencing were part of a broader movement towards criminal justice reform, and her work helped lay the foundation for future changes in federal sentencing policy. As a champion of justice, Jackson's legacy at the Sentencing Commission is one of thoughtful, moral leadership and a deep commitment to ensuring that the law serves all people equally.

Decisions

Ketanji Brown Jackson's tenure at the U.S. Sentencing Commission was marked by several critical decisions and initiatives that showcased her commitment to fair and equitable sentencing practices. One of the most significant was her work on the Commission's decision to retroactively apply the Fair Sentencing Act. This move had a profound impact on thousands of individuals who had been serving harsh sentences for crack cocaine offences.

The decision to apply the Fair Sentencing Act retroactively was challenging. There were concerns about the potential impact on public safety and the logistical difficulties of reviewing and potentially reducing thousands of sentences. However, Jackson strongly advocated for retroactive application, arguing that justice required those sentenced under the old, unjust guidelines to be allowed a fairer sentence.

This decision was emblematic of Jackson's broader approach to sentencing reform. She believed that the law should be applied consistently and equitably, and she was willing to tackle complex and controversial issues to ensure that justice was served. Her work on the Fair Sentencing Act was a clear demonstration of her commitment to addressing the systemic inequities that had long plagued the U.S. criminal justice system.

In addition to her work on drug sentencing, Jackson played a vital role in the Commission's efforts to reform the sentencing guidelines for economic crimes. Recognizing the complexity of these offences and the varying degrees of harm they caused, she pushed for policies that would allow for more tailored and proportionate sentences. This was a significant departure from the more rigid guidelines that had previously been in place, and it reflected Jackson's belief in the importance of judicial discretion.

One of the most notable cases that Jackson worked on during her time at the Commission involved the sentencing guidelines for fraud offences. The Commission had long struggled with how to appropriately sentence individuals convicted of white-collar crimes, particularly those involving large-scale fraud. Jackson's approach was to advocate for guidelines that took into account the specific circumstances of each case, including the defendant's intent, the level of harm caused, and the need for restitution. This approach was designed to ensure that sentences were fair and reflective of the seriousness of the offence.

Jackson's work on the Commission also extended to the issue of mandatory minimum sentences. She was a vocal critic of these sentences, arguing that they often resulted in excessively harsh penalties that did not consider each case's individual circumstances. Her support was crucial to the Commission's attempts to suggest modifications to the federal sentencing guidelines that would provide judges more latitude in situations where the mandated minimums were considered unfair.

At the U.S. Sentencing Commission, Jackson was known for her thoughtful and conscientious approach to sentencing reform. She was unafraid to tackle complex and controversial issues, and a deep commitment to justice and fairness always guided her. Her work had a lasting impact on federal sentencing practices, and she is widely regarded as one of the most influential voices in the movement for criminal justice reform.

Jackson's tenure at the Commission was a critical period in her career that solidified her reputation as a champion of justice and an advocate for fairness in the criminal justice system. Her efforts influenced federal sentencing guidelines and established the framework for future changes that still affect the lives of thousands of people nationwide.

Chapter 4

Rising Through the Ranks

When Ketanji Brown Jackson was appointed judge in the U.S. District Court for the District of Columbia in 2013, she was allowed to address some of the most important legal precedents and contemporary concerns. With President Obama's nomination, she entered a new phase of her legal career, one in which her choices would have a direct bearing on the interpretation of federal law and the lives of countless others.

Jackson's legal philosophy was first shown in Pierce v. District of Columbia. Jackson decided that benefited a deaf prisoner who had been refused access to interpreters who spoke sign language. Given that Jackson stressed that prisoners maintain fundamental rights, such as immunity from discrimination based on their condition, the decision was a significant win for the rights of people with disabilities. Her choice demonstrated her dedication to ensuring that everyone is treated with respect and dignity according to the law, regardless of their circumstances.

During her tenure on the District Court, the American Federation of Government Employees v. FLRA case gained noteworthy attention. Jackson's thorough ruling, in this case, upheld public sector labor organizations' rights to collective bargaining. The Federal Labor Relations Authority's decision to impose a new criterion restricting the extent of collective bargaining was at the center of the issue. Jackson's decision overturned the new norm, reaffirming the significance of labor rights and the need for government organizations to follow established legal protocols when implementing significant policy changes. Her choice demonstrated her commitment to upholding workers' rights and her conviction in the significance of ethical labor practices.

Jackson's judicial philosophy was often characterized by a delicate balancing act between a rigorous devotion to the law and a profound awareness of the practical consequences of her decisions. Jackson heard the case of Willis v. Gray, in which a long-serving public school teacher claimed that he was unfairly fired because of prejudice based on his age and colour. Jackson's decision allowed the teacher's discrimination allegations to be pursued, underscoring her dedication to ensuring that people can seek justice, mainly when it seems their rights have been violated.

Tyson v. Brennan, another landmark decision, showed Jackson's commitment to defending employees' rights to practice their religion in the workplace. In one example, a postal worker claimed he was subjected to discrimination because he listened to gospel music at work. However, other staff members were free to listen to secular music. Jackson rejected the Postal Service's request to dismiss the case because he believed that all workers should be treated fairly, regardless of their religious convictions. This decision upheld the principle that discrimination in the workplace, in whatever form, ought to be investigated and dealt with by the legal system.

Committee on the Judiciary v. McGahn was among Jackson's most well-known cases on the District Court. In this instance, former White House Counsel Don McGahn was served with a subpoena by the House Judiciary Committee as part of its investigation into possible obstruction of justice by President Trump. According to Jackson's famous opinion, which included the statement "Presidents are not kings," McGahn could not use his claims of absolute immunity as justification for ignoring the subpoena. The idea that nobody is above the law—not even the President—was strongly affirmed by this ruling. Jackson's decision received high appreciation for its clarity and tenacious upholding of the law.

Jackson's decisions on the District Court were distinguished by their careful consideration of the law and strong sense of justice throughout her tenure. She addressed every case with a dedication to justice, making sure that her rulings were both solid legally and taking into account the repercussions for society. Her work on the District Court established her as a principled and analytical jurist who was not hesitant to take on challenging legal matters, which prepared the basis for her future career as a judge.

Appellate Power

In 2021, Ketanji Brown Jackson's judicial career took another significant step forward when she was appointed to the U.S. Court of Appeals for the District of Columbia Circuit, often referred to as the second most powerful court in the United States. This court has heard numerous of the country's most significant regulatory and administrative law matters. Jackson's nomination was seen as an acknowledgment of her aptitude for higher judicial positions and her mastery of the legal system.

American Federation of Government Employees v. FLRA was among the first cases she heard on the D.C. Circuit, and it was in this case, she once again defended labor rights. This time, she wrote an opinion overturning a Trump administration rule restricting federal workers' ability to engage in collective bargaining. Her choice demonstrated her continued support for labor rights and her conviction that judicial supervision is necessary to guarantee that government acts adhere to the law.

Jackson made important administrative and environmental rulings while serving on the D.C. Circuit. Jackson decided against the Government of Guam v. United States, a complicated issue concerning ecological remediation obligations favouring Guam. The main question in the case was whether the U.S. government was responsible for paying for the remediation of a landfill that was used as a military dumping site. Jackson's decision, which allowed Guam's action against the U.S. government to go forward, was a significant win for the island and demonstrated her ability to handle complicated legal matters reasonably and precisely.

Uber Technologies v. Equal Rights Center was another critical case. Uber's adherence to the Americans with Disabilities Act (ADA) was contested in this case. According to the plaintiffs, Uber violated the Americans with Disabilities Act (ADA) by not having any wheelchair-accessible cars in Washington, D.C. Jackson's decision made it possible for the lawsuit to proceed and emphasized the need for technology businesses to abide by federal handicap rules just as conventional transportation providers do. Her choice strongly indicated that contemporary commerce companies are subject to customary legal obligations.

Jackson addressed the subject of law enforcement personnel's qualified immunity in Patterson v. United States. An Occupy D.C. protester filed a lawsuit against the police, arguing that they had wrongfully arrested him and that his First Amendment rights had been infringed. Jackson's decision rejected the police's argument of qualified immunity, stating that the arrest was probably unlawful since it was made only based on the demonstrator's words. Her dedication to upholding constitutional rights and making sure that law enforcement is held responsible for activities that violate those rights was shown by her ruling.

Jackson's opinions on the D.C. Circuit were characterized by a strong regard for the rule of law and a dedication to ensuring that everyone was treated fairly and equally under the law. Knowing that her rulings would often create significant legal precedents, she addressed each case with the same rigor and care that had defined her work on the District Court but with an additional layer of responsibility.

A pivotal time in Jackson's judicial career occurred when she was on the D.C. Circuit. It allowed her to discuss some of the most important legal matters of the day and hone her judicial philosophy in an environment that often served as a springboard to the Supreme Court. Her decisions on the D.C. Circuit cemented her status as one of the most reputable judges in the federal system by demonstrating her ability to manage complex and consequential matters reasonably and accurately.

Chapter 5

Making History

The morning of February 25, 2022, dawned like any other for Ketanji Brown Jackson, but her life would change forever by the end of the day. President Joe Biden officially nominated her to the United States Supreme Court, marking a historic moment as she became the first Black woman to be selected for the nation's highest Court. This nomination culminated in a distinguished legal career and the beginning of an intense and scrutinized confirmation process that would captivate the nation.

The journey to confirmation was fraught with challenges, reflecting the polarized political climate of the time. Jackson's nomination came at a critical juncture in American history, with the Supreme Court at the centre of debates on issues ranging from abortion rights to voting laws. As the country's first Black female nominee to the Supreme Court, Jackson's confirmation hearings were a test of her qualifications and a reflection of the broader struggles for racial and gender equality in America.

When her nomination was announced, Jackson faced a barrage of public scrutiny. Every aspect of her life, from her judicial record to her personal beliefs, was under the microscope. The confirmation hearings, held by the Senate Judiciary Committee, were a marathon of questions that spanned several days. Jackson was interrogated by senators from both parties on a broad variety of subjects, including her opinions on constitutional interpretation and her previous decisions on divisive matters.

One of the most intense moments of the hearings came when Jackson was questioned about her previous rulings on child pornography cases. Critics accused her of being too lenient in her sentencing, while supporters argued that she had adhered to federal sentencing guidelines and exercised appropriate judicial discretion. Composed and articulate, Jackson defended her record, emphasizing her commitment to following the law and ensuring justice was served in every case she handled.

Despite the rigorous questioning, Jackson's calm demeanour and extensive legal knowledge won her praise from many quarters. Her responses reflected her deep understanding of the law and her ability to remain poised under pressure—a trait that would serve her well on the nation's highest Court. Her confirmation hearings also highlighted the historic nature of her nomination, as many senators and commentators pointed out the significance of her potential to bring a new perspective to the Supreme Court.

The road to confirmation took work. The Senate Judiciary Committee deadlocked in an 11-11 vote along party lines, forcing the full Senate to take a procedural vote to advance her nomination. Ultimately, the Senate confirmed Jackson on April 7, 2022, by a vote of 53-47, with three Republican senators joining all 50 Democrats in supporting her. The final vote was a moment of profound significance for Jackson and the entire nation. As she was sworn in on June 30, 2022, the United States celebrated the first Black woman to serve on the Supreme Court—a milestone that would resonate for generations.

The confirmation journey of Ketanji Brown Jackson reflected both the progress America has made and the challenges that remain. It was proof of her perseverance, dedication to justice, and unwavering belief in the principles of the Constitution. Her nomination and eventual confirmation were not just personal achievements; they were historic milestones that symbolized a broader movement towards greater representation and inclusion at the highest levels of the American judiciary.

Public Perception

Ketanji Brown Jackson's nomination to the Supreme Court sparked many reactions across the political spectrum, reflecting the deep divisions in American society. For many, her nomination was a long-overdue step toward greater diversity and representation on the Court. For others, it was a moment of intense political debate, as her judicial philosophy and past rulings became focal points in a broader conversation about the future direction of the Court.

The significance of Jackson's nomination was immediately recognized by civil rights organizations, legal scholars, and the media. Many praised President Biden's decision to nominate a highly qualified Black woman, noting that Jackson's background as a public defender, a federal judge, and a member of the U.S. Sentencing Commission brought a unique and much-needed perspective to the Court. Her nomination was seen as a victory for those who had long advocated for a more inclusive judiciary that better reflected the diversity of the American population.

However, the political dynamics surrounding her nomination were complex. While some celebrated the historic nature of her selection, others viewed it through the lens of partisan politics. Critics, particularly from conservative circles, expressed concerns about Jackson's judicial philosophy, fearing that her presence on the Court could tilt its balance on critical issues such as abortion, gun rights, and affirmative action. Her previous rulings amplified these concerns, which were scrutinized for any indication of how she might approach these contentious issues as a Supreme Court Justice.

The confirmation hearings became a battleground where these political dynamics played out in real time. Supporters of Jackson emphasized her qualifications and commitment to upholding the rule of law, while opponents sought to portray her as an activist judge who might legislate from the bench. The intense media coverage of the hearings only heightened the sense of drama, with every moment dissected and analyzed for its potential impact on the final confirmation vote.

Broader social and cultural factors also shaped public perception of Jackson's nomination. For many Black Americans, her nomination was a source of immense pride, a symbol of progress in a country still grappling with the legacies of racism and inequality. Jackson's rise to the highest Court in the land was seen as a validation of the hard-fought gains of the civil rights movement and a beacon of hope for future generations.

Yet, her nomination also underscored the ongoing struggles for racial and gender equality in America. The fact that Jackson was the first Black woman ever nominated to the Supreme Court in its more than two centuries was a cause for celebration and a sobering reminder of the barriers that historically excluded people of colour and women from the highest echelons of power. This duality was reflected in the public discourse, where her nomination was simultaneously hailed as a breakthrough and critiqued as a long-overdue correction.

As the confirmation process unfolded, it became clear that Jackson's nomination was more than just filling a seat on the Supreme Court. It was a referendum on the state of American democracy, a test of the nation's commitment to diversity and inclusion, and a reflection of the deep ideological divides that continue to shape its political landscape. The confirmation of Ketanji Brown Jackson was not just a victory for her; it was a moment of reckoning for the country as a whole.

In the end, Jackson's successful confirmation represented a triumph of perseverance, skill, and integrity over the forces of division and partisanship. It was a powerful reminder that the arc of the moral universe, as Martin Luther King Jr. famously said, bends toward justice—though it does so slowly and with great effort.

As Ketanji Brown Jackson took her place on the Supreme Court, millions of Americans looked to her as a fresh beginning in the fight for equality and justice, and she carried their dreams and ambitions with her.

Chapter 6

In The Supreme Court

With her diverse experience as a former public defender, federal judge, and member of the U.S. Sentencing Commission, Ketanji Brown Jackson brought a new viewpoint to the U.S. Supreme Court, which was immediately apparent. Her dissents have been marked by a powerful articulation of her judicial philosophy. She often challenged the majority with arguments grounded in both historical context and contemporary justice.

A significant case from her first term was University of North Carolina v. Students for Fair Admissions (2023), in which the Supreme Court delivered a judgment criticizing the application of admissions criteria based on race. In this case, Jackson penned a powerful dissent, arguing that the majority's decision failed to consider the historical context of the 14th Amendment. Her main point was that the Amendment's framers weren't trying to establish race neutrality but rather to remedy the unique injustices that African Americans experienced after the Civil War. Jackson's dissent was deeply rooted in historical analysis, and she made a compelling case that race-conscious policies are consistent with the original intent of the Constitution's equal protection clause.

Jackson's dissent in this case highlighted her ability to engage with the conservative majority on their terms, using originalist arguments to make her case. This approach showcased her deep understanding of constitutional history and demonstrated her commitment to ensuring that the Court's decisions reflect the reality of America's ongoing struggles with racial inequality.

Another case Jackson impacted was Merrill v. Milligan (2023), a pivotal voting rights case. Here, Jackson's questioning during oral arguments was particularly striking. She challenged the state of Alabama's arguments for a "colour-blind" approach to redistricting, pointing out that such an approach ignores the historical and ongoing realities of racial discrimination in voting. Her questions were instrumental in framing the case regarding the broader history of voting rights and racial justice in America. Ultimately, the Court ruled in favour of the minority voters, with Jackson's contributions during oral arguments credited with influencing the outcome.

These early dissents and contributions in oral arguments have set the tone for Jackson's tenure on the Supreme Court. Her background as a public defender and her work on criminal justice reform issues has given her a unique perspective that prioritizes the lived experiences of marginalized communities and the historical context of the laws in question. This approach has made her a powerful voice in the Court, particularly in cases where racial justice issues are at stake.

Key Cases and Rulings

Beyond her dissents, Jackson's early rulings on the Supreme Court have further illustrated how her judicial philosophy, honed during her time in the lower courts, is applied in her new role. In 303 Creative LLC v. Elenis (2023), a case involving the clash between free speech and anti-discrimination laws, Jackson joined the dissenting opinion, arguing that the majority's decision to allow a business to refuse services to same-sex couples on free speech grounds undermined the principles of equality and nondiscrimination. Her position in this case reflected her broader commitment to protecting the rights of marginalized groups, a theme consistent with her earlier work as a judge.

Another significant ruling was her majority opinion in Delaware v. Pennsylvania and Wisconsin (2023), which dealt with the division of unclaimed financial assets between states. While the case was more technical than controversial, it marked Jackson's first majority opinion on the Court. Her clear and methodical reasoning in the argument was praised for its precision and attention to detail, qualities that have defined her judicial style throughout her career.

In United States v. Texas (2023), a case that dealt with the Biden administration's immigration policies, Jackson's involvement was again noteworthy. Although she did not author the majority opinion, her participation in the ruling aligned with her broader judicial philosophy of upholding federal authority in the context of immigration law. This stance reflects her belief in the importance of government action to protect vulnerable populations.

Consistent with her earlier judicial work, Jackson prioritized equality, justice, and the preservation of individual rights in her early rulings. However, her role on the Supreme Court has also required her to adapt her philosophy to the broader and more complex issues before the nation's highest Court. In doing so, Jackson has demonstrated her ability to grow into her role while remaining true to the principles guiding her throughout her legal career.

As Jackson continues her tenure on the Supreme Court, her early rulings and dissents have made it clear that she will be a formidable force on the bench. Her ability to articulate her views with clarity and conviction, coupled with her deep understanding of the law and its historical context, ensures that her impact on the Court will be felt for years to come.

Chapter 7

A Voice for the Voiceless

Ketanji Brown Jackson's commitment to civil rights and advocacy for marginalized communities have been consistent themes throughout her legal career. From her early days as a public defender to her recent role as a Supreme Court Justice, Jackson has been a staunch advocate for those who often find themselves without a voice in the legal system.

One of the most notable aspects of Jackson's advocacy is her focus on disability rights. While serving as a District Court judge, her ruling in Pierce v. District of Columbia (2015) stands out as a pivotal moment. In this case, Jackson ruled in favour of a deaf inmate who had been denied access to sign language interpreters while incarcerated. Jackson's decision was not just about enforcing the Americans with Disabilities

Act (ADA); it was a powerful statement on the rights of disabled individuals, particularly those in vulnerable situations such as incarceration. Her ruling underscored the principle that all individuals deserve equal protection and access under the law regardless of their circumstances.

Jackson's influence extended beyond her courtroom rulings. She has also used her platform to speak out on civil rights issues. In various public remarks, Jackson has underlined the need of representation within the judicial system and diversity. She has argued that a judiciary reflecting the nation's diversity is better equipped to deliver fair and equitable justice. Her speeches often draw on her experiences as a Black woman in a predominantly white legal field, providing a personal perspective that resonates with many.

Another critical area of Jackson's advocacy has been employment discrimination. Her ruling in Willis v. Gray (2020) allowed a long-serving public school teacher to proceed with his claims of age and race discrimination, emphasizing the need for individuals to have their day in court, particularly when their civil rights may have been violated. This case clearly illustrated Jackson's conviction in the need of keeping institutions responsible and ensuring that the rights of workers are safeguarded against discrimination.

Jackson's commitment to civil rights is also evident in her work on the U.S. Sentencing Commission, where she advocated for reforms that addressed the racial disparities in sentencing, particularly in drug-related offenses. Her work contributed to the retroactive application of the Fair Sentencing Act, which helped reduce the sentences of thousands of individuals, most of whom were Black or Latino. This work was part of a broader effort to make the criminal justice system more just and equitable, particularly for communities that harsh sentencing laws have disproportionately impacted.

Through her rulings, speeches, and advocacy work, Jackson has consistently demonstrated a commitment to advancing civil rights and protecting the rights of marginalized communities. Her work has had a profound impact on the lives of many, and her legacy as an advocate for justice continues to grow.

Influence

Ketanji Brown Jackson's impact on American law extends beyond her rulings and speeches. Her approach to jurisprudence, characterized by a deep commitment to justice and fairness, will likely have a lasting influence on the legal landscape in the United States.

One area where Jackson's influence is already being felt is in the realm of disability rights. Her rulings have set important precedents that reinforce the rights of disabled individuals, particularly in contexts where those rights have been historically neglected. The principles she has articulated in her rulings, such as the necessity of providing accommodations and ensuring equal access, will likely influence future cases and legal interpretations in this area. Legal scholars have noted that Jackson's approach could lead to a more robust application of the ADA in various contexts, from employment to education to incarceration.

Jackson's influence is also evident in her approach to issues of race and discrimination. Her rulings and public statements have emphasized acknowledging and addressing the historical and systemic factors contributing to racial disparities in the legal system. This perspective is particularly relevant in the ongoing debates over affirmative action, voting rights, and criminal justice reform. Jackson's views on these issues, rooted in a deep understanding of the law and the lived experiences of marginalized communities, will likely shape the future direction of American jurisprudence in these critical areas.

Moreover, Jackson's emphasis on the importance of judicial empathy—understanding the real-world impact of legal decisions on individuals and communities—represents a shift towards a more human-centered approach to jurisprudence. This perspective challenges the more traditional, detached approach to legal decision-making and advocates for a judiciary attuned to its rulings' social and human consequences. This method might lead to more equal decisions in social justice, civil rights, and human rights disputes.

Jackson's influence is also likely to extend to the broader legal community, particularly among younger lawyers and judges who see her as a role model for integrating advocacy and empathy into their work. Her example demonstrates that it is possible to be both a rigorous legal thinker and a passionate advocate for justice and that these two roles are not mutually exclusive. As Jackson's example inspires more lawyers and judges, her approach to the law could become more prevalent, leading to a judiciary that is more reflective of the diverse society it serves.

Ketanji Brown Jackson's work advocating for civil rights and influencing future jurisprudence significantly contribute to American law. Her commitment to justice, emphasis on the importance of diversity and representation, and empathetic approach to legal decision-making will likely shape the legal landscape for years to come. As her career continues, her impact will undoubtedly continue to grow, making her one of her generation's most influential legal figures.

Chapter 8

Beyond the Bench

Ketanji Brown Jackson's journey to becoming a Supreme Court Justice is deeply intertwined with the relationships she has cultivated throughout her life, particularly with her husband and children. These relationships have been a source of strength and inspiration, shaping her values and approach to her professional life.

Jackson met her husband, Patrick Jackson, while they were both students at Harvard. Patrick, a surgeon, has been a steadfast supporter of her career, providing the emotional and practical support that has enabled her to pursue her demanding legal job with confidence. Their relationship, grounded in mutual respect and shared values, has been a cornerstone of Jackson's life, allowing her to navigate the challenges of her career while maintaining a solid family life.

The couple married in 1996 and have two daughters, Talia and Leila, who have been a constant source of joy and motivation for Jackson. She has often spoken about the importance of being a role model for her daughters, showing them that pursuing a career at the highest levels is possible while being an involved and caring parent. This balancing act between career and family has required careful time management and prioritization. Still, it has also reinforced Jackson's belief in the importance of resilience, balance, and the support systems that enable individuals to thrive.

Jackson's closeness to her family has also affected her view on the necessity of representation and diversity within the legal profession. As a mother raising two daughters in a world where women and people of colour have historically been underrepresented in positions of power, Jackson is acutely aware of the impact that her career can have on the next generation. She has spoken about the significance of her role on the Supreme Court, not only in terms of the legal decisions she makes but also as a symbol of what is possible for young women, particularly those from marginalized communities.

The support and encouragement Jackson receives from her husband and daughters have also played a crucial role in her ability to remain grounded despite her many achievements. She often reflects on how her family keeps her focused on what truly matters, reminding her of the human impact of her work and the broader implications of the legal decisions she helps shape. This grounding influence has been vital in maintaining her humility and perspective, which have defined her approach to her personal and professional life.

Balance

For Ketanji Brown Jackson, the journey to the Supreme Court has been marked by professional achievements and the ongoing challenge of balancing her personal life with the demands of her career. As a mother, wife, and legal professional, Jackson has navigated the complexities of a life in the public eye while maintaining the core values that have guided her since childhood.

One of Jackson's most significant challenges is the constant balancing act between her professional responsibilities and her role as a mother. Raising two daughters while climbing the ranks of the legal profession required careful time management, a strong support network, and a commitment to being present for her family despite the demands of her career. Jackson has often spoken about the importance of being a role model for her daughters, showing them that pursuing a demanding job and being an involved and supportive parent is possible.

Jackson's experience of balancing family life with her career has also given her a unique perspective on the issues faced by working parents, particularly women. She has acknowledged the pressures and sacrifices of trying to excel in both areas and has used her platform to advocate for policies that support work-life balance. In her speeches and public appearances, Jackson has often highlighted the need for more flexible work arrangements and better support systems for working parents, drawing on her own experiences to underscore the importance of these issues.

Another aspect of Jackson's life that has shaped her professional ethos is her ability to remain grounded despite her many achievements. Throughout her career, Jackson has maintained a strong sense of humility, often attributing her success to the support of her family and the opportunities provided to her by mentors and colleagues. This humility is reflected in her approach to her work on the Supreme Court, where she has consistently emphasized the importance of listening, learning, and being open to different perspectives.

Jackson's experiences have also influenced her approach to the law more directly. For example, her understanding of the challenges faced by working parents has informed her views on cases related to employment discrimination, parental leave, and workplace accommodations. Her empathy for those who struggle to balance work and family life has led her to advocate for legal protections that support these individuals, ensuring that the law reflects the realities of modern life.

Despite the obstacles of managing a demanding job with family commitments, Jackson has found ways to integrate her values into her professional life. She has often spoken about the importance of being true to oneself, even when facing external pressures. This commitment to authenticity has driven her career, guiding her decisions on and off the bench.

Ketanji Brown Jackson's personal life has profoundly impacted her professional ethos. The values instilled in her by her family, her experiences as a mother and wife, and her commitment to balancing her personal and professional responsibilities have all shaped her approach to the law and her role as a Supreme

Court Justice. As she continues navigating the challenges of her career, Jackson's personal life remains a source of strength and inspiration, guiding her work and contributions to the broader legal landscape.

Chapter 9

Conclusion

Ketanji Brown Jackson's journey to the U.S. Supreme Court is more than a spectacular personal accomplishment; it is a compelling example of tenacity, intelligence, and a genuine devotion to justice. Her career, from a little girl with enormous hopes to one of the nation's most powerful legal brains, inspires innumerable others who see in her a mirror of their own desires. However, Jackson's narrative is not simply about personal triumph; it is about the more significant influence of her efforts on American culture and the legal environment.

Throughout her career, Jackson has repeatedly exhibited a deep knowledge of the power of the law to bring about change. Her verdicts in the District and Appeals Courts were characterized by rigorous attention to detail and a devotion to justice, frequently giving voice to people who the legal system had disenfranchised. As a Supreme Court Justice, she has maintained this effort, bringing her judicial philosophy to some of the most critical problems of our day, from civil rights to criminal justice reform. Her dissents, in particular, have been eloquent demonstrations of her trust in the law as an instrument for promoting justice and equality.

Jackson's effect goes beyond her court rulings. As the first Black woman to serve in this post, her position on the Supreme Court is a significant signal of progress. It sends a message that the highest levels of the American Court are starting to reflect the diversity of the country it serves. This is not merely a symbolic win; it has genuine repercussions for the sorts of viewpoints and experiences brought to bear in the Court's deliberations, altering the path of American law for centuries to come.

However, Jackson's most important legacy resides in her ability to manage the demands of her job with her dedication to her family and her principles. Her tale is one of tenacity, forged by the trials of pursuing a road that has not always been simple. Yet, despite it all, she has stayed grounded, deriving strength from her connections and keeping loyal to the beliefs that have guided her from infancy. This balance between the personal and the professional is a monument to her character. It gives a compelling example to those striving to make a difference in their lives and communities.

As we look to the future, it is apparent that Ketanji Brown Jackson's imprint on the Supreme Court and on American law will be substantial. Her legal acumen, devotion to justice, and compassionate approach to the law will continue to define her choices and, in turn, the society we live in. But beyond her legal legacy, Jackson leaves a legacy of hope—a notion that no matter the hurdles, it is possible to accomplish great things while keeping true to one's beliefs and supporting the people who matter most.

In the years to come, as Jackson continues to leave her imprint on the Supreme Court, her legacy will likely inspire future generations of attorneys, judges, and activists. She symbolizes not only the progress we have accomplished but also the work that still has to be done to establish a more fair and equal society. Her narrative is a reminder that the battle for justice is continuous and that every one of us, in our own way, may contribute to that cause.

Made in the USA
Las Vegas, NV
04 September 2024